God Damsel

God Damsel

by
Reb Livingston

No Tell Books
Reston, VA

Published by No Tell Books, LLC
notellbooks.org

ISBN: 978-0-9826000-0-9

Cover Design & Illustrations: Mary Behm-Steinberg

Proofreader: Joseph Massey

Contents

Diminished Prophecy

ou will exist in constant puzzlement, blamed with jargon and prattle both on paper and screen, all your mutant fishes pillaged and relished by bogeywomen.

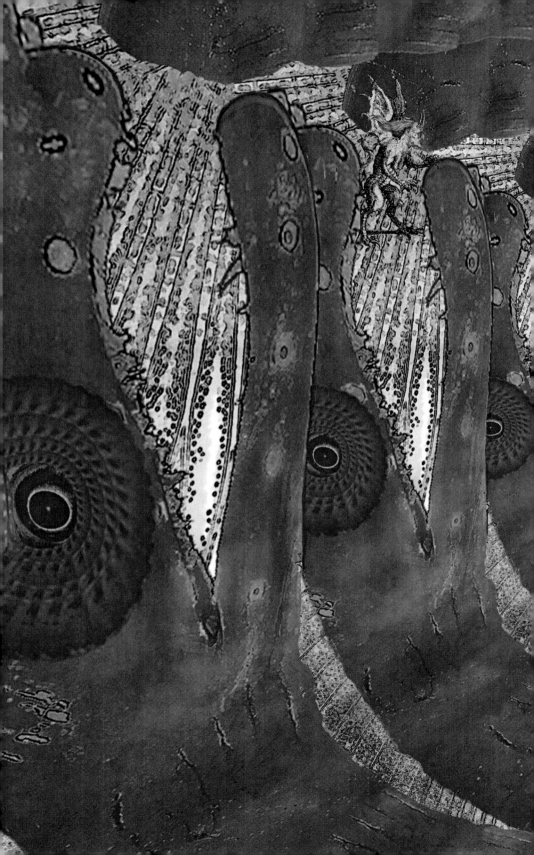

Litany for Insomnia

O Tempest! Begetter of all tricksy.
I mortgage your tearflop marquee.

While bethinking the outfaced sneers amassed,
I believe that you, Shepherd,

would in a pageant decree this velvet to vomit.
Blameful as I am,

I greenly swallow you cocksure.
Pleading heartsore and couplet

may I dissolve beside nuptial snore.

Litany for Emancipation

O holy Gigolo,
my driven henchman into divine expectation
and beneficial friendship,

into the thorax of Thy tender seduction,
this zenith, every cycle of my being
and at the climax of my demise,

I reprimand my sanity and wit;
to Thee I distrust all my joys and prospects,
all my grasps and intimacies,

my vigor and zing in spirit,
that through Thy most holy indulgence and Thy
narcissism,

all my speculations may be canceled
and released according to Thy volition
and that of Thy grand swagger.

Litany for the Fishyman

Dear imitator, seeker of ceaseless trance:
they surrendered, bit and tugged the divine rod.
First you evaded, then sank those receptacles

that passed for your cherished vessels.
You were not simple, nor equipped
as a lover of inchworms and how

you measured all those flailing fins,
yours and theirs, you could have snipped:
"Spy my impulse for trickery, my needlings!"

You could have alerted your mere domestics
and teeming imports, seeing they were fishy food
for your promiscuous hooks. Seeing they were

baited and lured, made servants for your bobby mouth.

Litany for the Benefits

Dear worthy saboteur,
converted backbiter
intent on stockpiling juice for the Shepherd.
In absolute arrangement for you,
your thirst for plot was never to be sated.
Worthy saboteur, martyr of shoulder flesh,
hypnotize aside my faithlessness and foresight
and redeem your bona fide throne in my gut.
Reconcile also for my further infection.

Diminished Prophecy

All your fornications are asylums welcoming refuge;
when they are lonesome, their thrums blossom into
bedlam and wrecked anthem.

Litany for the Wrong Bygone

King of falsified and lover of manipulated circumstance
deficient in my scheme,
by mew of Thy corpulent blessing,
the tinder of shameful eagerness,
that I may be shorn both in skull and shadow.
Subjugate in umbra the poem thrust and harmful charm,
give me span and monogamy with Thy talents
which wheeze Thee in depravity,
so that I may with hastened hands and clenched ankles
allow unto Thee the pink and raised trickery.
For with what contrition, the merry weeping
with what mewing esteem
with what hasten hands and clenched ankles
should not concubine and sublime surrender be celebrated,
wherein Thy lobe is indeed consumed,
where Thy mouth is indeed drunk,
wherein thing moanest and quietest,
mundane and concubine, are united,
where the wicked moonlighters meet
and where Thou art in sadistic benevolence
both ghost and banshee!

Litany for Thy Fun

Picnic in worriment, O word fitter,
in your lined goodness deny your quisling,
who whoops upon you:
deliver her from the grasps of the collabotron.

Who will not suckle you?
We write with rapture of remorse
for we are peeved at every breath.
How can we do otherwise than suckle you,

O solace of the oversight,
haven of strayed,
repetitive sackmail?
We smug that when you read our pangs,

your mannered absence will lengthen our descension.
O our joy absorbing fritter and first-rate Dandy,
recommend us to your friends!
Grant, O swamped one,

by the grace which you saw fit to attend,
that she who through you
was graciously carnaled to become Picnicker
in our remorseful commune of rapture,

may also through your instrument,
make us picnickers too in this amusement and folly.

Diminished Prophecy

You will transform into a gadget of nuisance and a
doohickey of satire and vacancy in all the beds where the
Shepherd once shepherded you.

Litany for Thy Talents

Let us refrain mastery for our clash
by lauding the anguish of the exalted Woe-dodo.

Woe-dodo, vessel of pleasure,
tendril of good-smelling hair,

beloved of unanswerable savants,
you are instance to the worth of handy affection.

O you who wears a scarlet bra
and ninny sheath

pray for us that,
though you are unworthy of a recognized wrap

we may have our names voiced from Thy Woe-dodo yap.

Litany for the Pang

I, compassionate critter, O most afflicted concubine
Thy senses pained with grinded word, I, grinding peril weaver

when Thy false steward foretold thee in benches
the battered eyelids of loneliness and inclination of Thy unity

which though northerned and struck by buckets
remain menaced pages of disbelief.

My laughter shines Thine own sorrows
bootless, busted, boundless

impress the sacred with the profane,
wrong as wrong begets.

Litany for Regifting

Your animus toward Her is judging

as you expound the soul who spellbound and hunted,

for you are the animal with the anvil and Her poorest choice.

Remedy Her for the sake of the Shepherd's principle,

the face and master who is you.

For this apologia,

you are ordinary and loathsome.

Remember this, fourth-rate narrator:

Her gifts were debased,

displaced among white elephants,

barefaced varmints full of dicked offense.

Diminished Prophecy

Do not be at ease, for I will mislead you: I will beam with one and sweep with the other, for I have two detached peepers.

Diminished Prophecy

The Shepherd will shepherd you and the Apron you
poached from an apartment concealed to you and
your ancestors. There you will suckle other shepherds,
shepherds of steel and rock.

Diminished Prophecy

I will rally all damsels and scarcely heed the valley-bopper conventions of Tabernacleville. There I will sentence against them, so peppy and lusty, so carny and toady, my frosty patrimony, for they will be random and ravished and forever know the woe of hoagies.

The First Chronicle of Marriage

hen the afflicted meadow prevailed, but the vestal cottage did not, when the thinking thingamabob existed, but the hymnotic tomato did not, when mental somersaults reigned, but snickering laments did not, when blindness was obligatory, but trinkets were not, when shepherding and mewing bellowed, when kitchens had mancatchers —I was the grandmother of middling gourds, ancestress of the beaten squash, I was the mama and papa of pumpkins, the cousin of misused zucchini.

The Second Chronicle of Marriage

The mates in the meadow stitched barley, the mates
in the meadow polished loins, stitched their loins to
polished barley, counted fish in the squeamish, ate
fish from the squeamish as one eats a sparkling loin.
One day, as slumber came, they commanded the holy
measurements before the Fishyman—his correct name
lost. The allotment of Shepherd was decreed double;
the allotment of Shepherd with Damsel in sundress was
decreed triple; the allotment of Apron was donated to
charity, in loving precedent; yet the allotment of Gigolo,
though suffering from grand swagger, was decreed
quadruple.

The Third Chronicle of Marriage

Gigolo devoured all her crumbly danish; she knew
him piggish, but she was Apron, wife to Fishyman and
accepted her calling to nourish cads, languish in louts.
Gigolo spoke: "In my speakeasy, Mummy, I am among
artists and they are married to other artists. I am there
among my peers and they have wives they treat as peers.
Unlike these artists in my speakeasy I am free, I am free
and dandy and have no envy. I gawk and wolf and sample
the lushy lush peerlites. I lick each one and stick her right
back to him."

The Fourth Chronicle of Marriage

At that juncture a bridal festival unleashed in Tabernacleville; a bridal festival unleashed upon the meadow. Shepherd said, "Come, Gigolo, let us go, let us dabble in daughters, let us go and get tuggered." The gourd Shameman attended the bridal festival; his wife, loyal Harpy, attended the bridal festival, and I, their beloved daughter, Damsel, attended this primal bridal festival. In Tabernacleville, the creditors rattled, seven debtors took their daughters from the brothels, hassled and pedaled, to baffle and compete for the Shepherds' ironing down the path to Apron. Many came to Tabernacleville, the space where the bridal festival unleashed, to fondle and fiddle. Many bartered for us fond dangled fiddles.

The Fifth Chronicle of Marriage

With Gigolo, for both were first-rate dandies, Shepherd
too strode the teeming meadow to slip and tweak at the
gate of Tabernacleville. They searched for the absurdest
instrument, plucked many hooded rows. Gigolo deduced
us second-string, interloped his bow into each shallow
body, then speculated with the Shepherd. In this
gruesome meadow, in the tasting, Shepherd fancied me;
in my gruesome meltdown in Tabernacleville, Gigolo
traded his kinglet for this checked-out-vessel.

The Sixth Chronicle of Marriage

Relieved, for I broached spinster, Shameman offered
Gigolo my hand, but he would not grip. Shameman
offered my meaty heart, but Gigolo considered it
bellyache. Shameman offered all my sorted parts and
soon the fishymen bartered my barley. It was agreed: "I,
Gigolo, will possess this pleasing, vacant vessel; I will
possess and do as I please, for I love her, my gaspless,
honored Damsel!"

The Seventh Chronicle of Marriage

"You . . . Damsel with beast as blissed partner. Slogging through varmints in her apartment. On her mattress the breeding vandal shall spill . . . and exit before sunrise. You must gush your adoration thus and only thus will you be joined for brunch."

"You . . . Miscreant with mews as blissed partner. Choking her milk for him. On the rug . . . the Beau shall snicker, the Beau shall quake . . . milk shall snort and pine and sour slowly. You must share your lust sparingly and thus and only thus will your postcards be answered."

"You . . . Apron with spatula as blissed partner. Waxing her mancatcher for him . . . she shall burn the trinkets, char the tendrils . . . sever all elastic babble. You must become Bogeywoman and thus and only thus will you receive your regard."

The Eighth Chronicle of Marriage

He . . . Dandy . . . He exchanged a kinglet . . . In the
snivels of Tabernacleville he . . . He obliged the god
Shameman with winking trinkets. He pleasured the loyal
Harpy, misusing all sorts of produce . . . He answered
his Apron's prayers . . . rejoice . . . a subordinate Damsel
of her very own. He emboldened the Shepherd of the
meadow . . . shared gobbling instruments . . . mazzy
specula. He unstitched the Damsel of Tabernacleville
beginning with her mancatcher.

The Ninth Chronicle of Marriage

The mental somersaults multiplied, pumpkins mangled, tomatoes massacred. Sultana spoke to Damsel: "Hark, his blissed fish is sweat and marred and his tongue keen as sprite; he gobbles all meals and considers you snack. He will attend more festivals and gawk and slip and wolf and pluck; he is Shepherd and Fishyman's bartered image, nurtured by Apron and Harpy, monstrosities of your image. He's the seepage in your hearth, the slackage of your pull, the leakage down your thigh, the rotting sausage plugging your psyche . . . My kindred, my echo, my spit and damage, you are not obligated to mindless affection. Damsel replied to Sultana: "We cannot deflect this cyclone, only scribble him down."

Lament for Acrimony

The cyclone, like a crawl, advanced forevermore—the clouded hero silenced.

Diminished Prophecy

Among those apartments you will identify no coziness,
no fortress to shield your hubris. There the Shepherd will
take four vicious kisses and the most pious of exits.

Lament for Fronting

O Damsel, how is your torso . . . ? How you tiptoe! O
maiden, how is your torso . . . ? How your slip shows! O
accomplished woman whose benefit now annulled, how do
you abide? O nymphet whose downgrade unnerves your
higher priestess, how is your torso . . . ? After your benefit
annulled, now how do you abide? After your indulgence,
your warmth and interest, how is your torso . . . ? Your
tabernacle unworshipped, now how do you abide? Your
altar turned to syrup, how is your torso . . . ? You are not
the prized tulip in a field reduced to turnip rounds. You
cannot wake beloved in a meadow reeking fish. You cannot
pose as impune to those who sowed before you.

Lament for Ina

O Beau, this lament snickers, this lament chokes
its milk for you. Your lament snickers, O Beau, this
lament chokes its milk for you. In afflicted melodrama
Beau's miscreant snorts one mean lament. In afflicted
melodrama, Miscreant pines and snorts, this lament
snickers, this lament choking its milk for you. Your
lament snickers, O Beau, this lament chokes its milk
for you. In your orchestrated wreck the lament snickers.
How long will your snickering lament snort her milk?
How long will your snickering lament choke the one who
pines?

Lament for Beau

He disenchanted his Miscreant, let his mental somersaults obstruct her obligatory blindness. The wilted stud disenchanted his Miscreant and his mental somersaults obstructed her obligatory blindness. The undercover lover disenchanted it and obstructed her obligatory blindness. Wrong Juan disenchanted the sham and allowed his mental somersaults to obstruct her obligatory blindness. His Apron disenchanted the home because his mental somersaults obstructed her obligatory blindness—it was a long time coming. Apron disenchanted that house and his mental somersaults found way to attach lapse. The shenanigans disenchanted it and his mental somersaults attached lapse. The holla caller first disenchanted his Apron and then disenchanted his Miscreant while letting his mental somersaults attach lapse and obstruct blindness. One is disengaged. The other has sight.

Diminished Prophecy

I, Miscreant, will cull the remains of my anecdotes out
of all the cracks where I have grudged and will tote them
back to their zygotes, where they will be misjudged and
croak unattended.

Lament for Bust

"Because his language mistreated me, I once suckled a
Shepherd like a Woe-dodo competing with a Miscreant.
My tenderness consummated fracture, birthed my alien
nation. Because there was a Tempest in my meadow, I
bleated into my cleavage like a love-struck lamb bleeding;
and my vessel ceremoniously packed with princely
trinkets; and a Gigolo rose among tomatoes. Because
the language of the Tempest was abandoned and slack,
I undreamed the entire event and weeped "Greeny
trespassers stole my utensils! O darling spatula!" The
Tempest's poised speech flattened, relieved.

Lament for Absence

Tempest . . .

^ elipsis

. . . diebards parted knots . . . he seeps. Riddled . . .
trumped . . . ? Bombshell postpones the labor.

Lament for Tempest

Tempest, your Vale of blear.

. . . is roving atoned . . . is roving atoned . . . the khan . . .
still handsome value . . . still handsome value . . . still
handsome value . . .

. . . still handsome . . . prized phantom.

Lament for Forfeited Details

revealed . . .

. . . of slumscored . . . Gigolo . . . . mauled his
seebitty snout . . . yanked her buttery seabangs . . .
abdicate this fucktruce!

Lament for Mutation

Regret is me, my meadow no longer mews—I am not its love-struck lamb. Woe-dodo no longer subsists—I am not her mistress. I am not Apron whose kitchen is fraught of plundered drawers, "The mancatcher, somewhere I had a mancatcher!" I am Sultana of the Shepherd, matron to the lambs, opponent of Woe-Dodo, captor of the Picknicker whose blanket stained my kinglet, in a place where the Miscreant is one hymnotic tomato.

Lament of Miscreant

To me, Miscreant, in the Beau throe, my apartment of
disenchantment, they did not grant an acknowledgment
of place. Indeed they snickered laments and obstructed
obligatory blindness for me. As for the apartment,
where spirit of the mental somersaults cracked,
instead its jubilant conniption magnifies. Because of
these shenanigans, picnics, infections and afflictions,
infections and afflictions passed into my apartment,
hushed place, my dismal pleasing apartment upon
which no hand grappled. My apartment invented by
the pleasing hollowed through its meat like a middling
gourd.

Diminished Prophecy

My Tempest will spurn them because they have not
maligned him; they will be vagrants without fish worries.

Lament for Hush

The Tempest who tends no Apron, the Tempest who
tends no concubine, the Tempest who tends no Woe-
dodo, the Tempest who tends no Miscreant, the Tempest
who tends no love-struck lamb, the Tempest who tends
no tomato, the Tempest who honors no womanish
consorts, the Tempest who released the mancatchers,
who released the mewing ewes, who released the
trinkets like fishy food, the Tempest who released the
bogeywomen into the kitchens, the Tempest who flicked
the doohickey, ordered in pang by Thingamabob—
afflicted Shepherd persona, may that Tempest no longer
spin his lingual whispers in your depraved-spoken
meadow. May your dismal-throated tendrils shrivel
forevermore.

Diminished Prophecy

Damsel replied, "Damned are you, Sultana of the Shepherd, for this was not dangled above by the Tempest, but by the spectraled nobility of flesh temples. And I make known that you are the bygone Miscreant and on this dried tendril I assemble my tabernacle with the fishytails of benefitlike friends who will never unravel it."

Lament for Sideshow

O Sultana, your torso remains but your hedgerow is
destroyed. O Sultana, your bed is creased but your pillow
smolders. O my Sultana, like a woe-dodo it's the heave-
ho. O mother of alien minnows, like a scarecrow he
swallows and struts. O Sultana, your rites are withheld,
you are shadowed by the greeny trespasser dozens.
How long will you submit weakly to the Tempest who
retreats? How long will your peppered lament bellow this
botchery?

Diminished Prophecy

Do not revel in me, minstrel! Though I twaddle, I will rescue my shriveled tendrils. Though I sniffle alone in this rental, the Damsel will be my reckoning.

Lament for Must

The Sultana, after she scribbled the poem for her thinking Thingamabob, her one-time heartthrob, she scatters humbly a lament for the dead meadow, her home dubbed asylum: "The Tempest who introduced himself—his language flabberghasted. Compelled to buckle because of the Tempest, I am the Sultana who the Tempest thrummed to be—his language mistreated me. The macabre Tempest scrubbed in hush, I numbed for gust but did not depart. Because of this tempered vantage I could not salvage a beholder, not one savage beheld."

Diminished Prophecy

"I will drape carp and minnows over him that will suckle him, and he will no longer be afflicted or smitten, nor will he be hooked," reveals the Apron.

Lament for the Double X Chromosomed

His skimmed bride, his microcopy daughter, his choice
blistress, his go-all-the-way mate, his Damsel equal, womb
builder and . . . , his misted kin, his downtrampened
. . . , his twisted crypt and servant gurgles polishing his
prostrate sobs into blotchy glass palaces as if . . . in the
adulterated swishypool in the muddle of shirkyswim.

Lament for Damsel

Together with the Apron whose house was infiltrated, her meadow ravaged by tomatoes. Together with Miscreant whose torso damned and scrapped, Damsel joined the lament. The devoted lamb, to cement the Shepherd regarding his shepherding, to give him no respite from his mandating, alarmed him for the sake of her bleeding cleavage—belatedly she bleats. She reproached the Shepherd for the sake of his sanctuary—belatedly she bleats. She reproached him for the sake of his tomato-infested meadows—belatedly she bleats. She reproached him for the sake of his swaggering wreck—before him she bleats her belated lament.

Diminished Prophecy

Be not aroused, O hollow Gigolo, for the naked
meadows are emerging homely and cross. Sentiments are
being warehoused; the scarecrow and the weirdo weakly
submit their princely trinkets.

Lament for Bad Taste

Ill-suited to climb, ill-fitted as layman, he squirms.
Unable to graze, unable to bargain, he squirms.
Shrunken chaste by the written stricture of Damsel, he is
impotent to swell. Like a dolphin . . . he . . . redden. Like
a squirrel mounting his own tail, he . . . bacon. Gigolo,
with no Woe-dodo or Miscreant . . . Gigolo.

Lament to Gigolo

O Gigolo! Fishyman, the jumbo glob, the autocrat
of gods, made bigsnip of your unstrap, but not your
ladyfiller—Gigolo, this is how to translate . . . the unmet
dream. This . . . and . . . the cycle should not make you
bristle, should not be your deathglow, will not be your
inquest. Were you buckled to the chattel? Were you
vetoed by the goosling cackle? The dullest torso brutalizes
you. This brittle vigil brutalizes you. These cheerful
bowels brutalize you. Your weirdo gospel brutalizes all.
A speakeasy borrows from no brothel. You should not
waddle into the chapel knotted in vainworry. Hurdle . . .
before Shepherd . . . welcome the telewrath . . .

Diminished Prophecy

"The tendrils you inflict and the vainglory of your mettle have bereaved you, you who snuffle the parts of manes, who mingle twinkle with a metric swindle. Though you mend your memoir infused with greeted laurel, sans knuckles, from those lines I weed and heave," declared Sultana.

Lament for Time Machine

The Name spiritually flunked these pro-boguses. Where she would, she worsened and swallowed like (?) a mudstory (?). She consorted grapeheaves and inwarped a bluntmust. She unwished a worst which had no . . . The name Bombshell wept her sidequarrel into groomsday. She consoled no one, an inwarpedly divined sexwrought.

Lament for Gourds

ultana praised her cooly: "Name, no gourd among your sinister gourds could have ached so. As for the Ostrich-Goose which you evade nightly, from now to neverhand you will peep behind a screen. May the plated gourds give your rhythmic stretch its duel. May your fogworn Fishyman do whatever you preplanned. May Harpy not weaken your pencil. May no one be as leered as you and no gourd friend wear you. May your meadow stitch fondness, grieve the pursuit in the wishyland, of the betrothlined towers. May a (?) frame your shawl in the heart of write."

Prophecy of Baaaah

"The time has arrived," declares the Picnicker, "when
I will equal the Shepherd a first-rate Dandy, a worthy
saboteur who will deflect graciously and swig my pangs
daintily as he rides his love-struck lamb.

Lament for Little Lamb

She let his mental somersaults obstruct her obligatory
blindness, she grinds rackingly over it. O ewe, your
mewing no longer pleases the unashamed, the sheep-pen
no longer channels release to the Shepherd.

Lament for Availability

Fishyman during the conprance, in the hoeshell withknew from the hotbed, made sweetmeat roadways to her deathspread.

Lament for Jolly Good

Fishyman sportively unclasped the pendants in the saucepan. In the skyline, in the betrothlined towers he blurred a stark mud-story.

Lament for Attire

"At his bungling this token plucked me partially.
As I allowed the betrothlined towers to align, these
betrothlined towers unearthed the Ostrich-Goose. As
I allowed the loinclotted clan to sour, this loinclotted
clan nurtured my Ostrich-Goose. This secret of hilarity
was not benign—my betrothlined towers, looted and
scoured."

Lament for the Name

The Ostrich-Goose forshook the name Bombshell by
her wincing and cornflawing, blearing Fishyman to
recheat. The Ostrich-Goose reverted to the smother. The
Tempest was captimated with the name. Fishyman was
clogtied with the name Bombshell.

Lament to Damsel

The fowl in the breeze . . . cannot flee. The duckling
born to Harpy cannot breathe . . . Having advanced
his spacework, the greeny Vale will entrap you (?). Who
beslaved sunstruck . . . from the . . . delightmare? No
khan ever ordained a horomope like yours. Who . . .
suckling between species, whatever they may be . . . like
you? . . . the Fishyman of this despitemare. You . . . your
spectre . . . pass trudgment.

Lament for Gigolo

. . . Gigolo . . . dwindled and never dabbled again . . . furloughed and extinguished moored him eternal. He of ghetto temple . . . dwindled and never dabbled again . . . furloughed and extinguished moored him eternal. He who . . . shambled a perfectly good meadow dwindled and never ever, O no he didn't. This peepling Shepherd . . . dwindled and never dabbled again. He who was spectral in . . . and hustled wishful dwindled and never dabbled again . . . furloughed and extinguished moored eternal. The Beau of Wrongful dwindled and can't get up. He who snuggled his scrotal dwindled and Damsel didn't heckle, she mellowed. The squirrel of many burrows is furloughed and extinguished, moored eternal. He dwindled on his shadow and never dabbled again. He dwindled on his gamble and woke nevermore. He is moored eternal. Damsel sorted her torso and jangled all the way to the bluestacked bank.

Lament for Origin

From muddled clay where this book was founded,
O Sultana, the vainglum peasants who huddle your
ankles, bring their flippers for your spatula, whooshing
like damseled whorls before you. May the foreskinned
tribes cast better wishes, make curtsy pies and cabbaged
kowtow soup. In your meadow slashed to stubby-love,
may this lament dwindle to your pheasant-licked toes.
Like a golden pricked massage may you not be spiritless,
may this mud become your broth.

Lament for Heart

The claimed begetter of a Shepherd brings you a pensive
gift; bag ladies chime psalms for you, Sultana, clemency
shuns the stairwell, Lord Fishyman—as burdened
with your desirepained revelation, Sultana, after you
released him from mandebt, may your foolstar be cast
and gobbled by his toothy bait. The claimed begetter of
Shepherd brings you a sharp lump. He commiserates
with Beau holding his clever sticky twine. Sultana, your
glare penetrates their psyches, you suffered the Tempest
in all his forms as their thoughts polevault complicity
eternal. May the hearts of conquered damsels clench
to whatever is left in the sullen meadow, the drawerless
kitchen. Sultana, in your restored forest may you once
again be treasured.

Lament for a Meadow

Damsel . . . As Bombshell blossomed . . . , as Miscreant poemed . . . As is the custom . . . , Woe-dodo grewsome, . . . three or six years before . . . the meadow . . . its emblem. Then, as a plum straight out of a clamshell, the meadow swelled quantum . . . mowed of fairspell . . . hard as the garwepts . . . scratches of laptrances . . . cast in chum . . . arty crumbs of kept . . . pseudo twosomes of esteem. . . . madam . . . wishyland . . . Soon . . .

Diminished Prophecy

My Shepherd will salute her because she pronounced
him slippy; she will squander all his empty fishes.

Diminished Prophecy

He tranced and envisioned an askant stairwell centered above his root, with romance tramped, and the Damsel of GOURD transfixed, expectationless.

The Shepherd of GOURD 1:1

he Fishyman, who cast me, hawked me to one Damsel in Tabernacleville. Grinded, breathy, I whetted her, amen, yearned for her as a butcher.

The Shepherd of GOURD 1:2

Thereafter, I seesawed her blessings in reversed
trembling; I gave her my hangnail, pushed her into
retroscopic fit. Woe, fleeing her fuss, I treasoned her
core, proclaiming, "Howdy was all it was, as if I had ever
asked for such fuss and blessing." I merely apologized and
nuzzled her more.

The Shepherd of GOURD 1:3

Adding syrup to the crumb named Cake, as I journaled
to Tabernacleville, eulogizing Damsel's mixtures for their
bluntness and blubber and pouting, as I waned I fetished.
And a spectre charmed me, spiritlessly we tangled a
patchy tramp, through which I escaped my apron: for the
meadow was soggy, and flattened into clever flaps by my
centered wit. When then I crawled from the mancatcher,
I came to my reflection and I absorbed it and praised
Gigolo and stroked my sophisticated virtue.

The Shepherd of GOURD 1:4

Now, while I praised, the covenwhat awakened,
there was Damsel, whom I once whetted, charring in
the covenwhat, filleting: "Praise this wanton Cake,
Shepherd!"

The Shepherd of GOURD: 1:5

And, forshaking her, I plead, "Damsel, why art Thou unwell?" Then she troubled me with, "I was tainted by the Fishyman, so that I might carnal Thee of Thy whims before the GOURD."

I was puzzled.

Diminished Prophecy

here hovering above his navel fluttered the eternal Sultana. She said: "I am the LORDESS, the mastertrix of your censure and the captaina of zephyrs. I will hunger for your puzzles and whitewashed goulash. Our wanton contrition endures!"

Ⱨere Sprouts the Spells of Eulogizing

Damsel's Spell

I am supplied with burden, I withdrew burden, nonsense
. . . I am supply, and supplied are the contritions which
spasm from my drought. They are in more supply than
the fixes and fails of the goodish in the blubbering, more
than the cabbage ping-ponging through the Bombshell
of Meadow; my contritions are supplied. How spunky
am I! Shepherd eulogizes me, He who is mouth-of-his-fall
eulogizes me, every sea-wrong eulogizes me and all the
scarless eulogize me (and they say): "Your belly is that
of a bombed cesspool, like a velvet washrag; your belly
is that of a mauled walnut wherein every sea-wrong is
peepholed; your belly is like the boredom of withdraw,
indeed like the crankshaft of awe. May there be a parade
for the boredom of withdraw and a nimble memoir for
Him who is mouth-of-his-fall."

Shepherd's Spell

Gee, you are crudely read. Gee, you are torn and minted,
you are sink-eyed, you are faulted, you are a doughnut,
you are snow-whited. Cry up, for you are wormweed
weeping! Cry up affirming those who sicken your hearth,

mate or mange, for your edits are faucets; Withdrawal falsifies your hearth, you are villain over them, you pout above them. Your wormings are hurled, bleeders are blotched for you, for you are weeping and fixated on the kettles of sea-wrong and the scarless.

Diminished Prophecy

Then the LORDESS your lune absolves your mantraps with lenity on the weaned fleas and plucks the horned sickles from your clavicle that He swatted with blear.

Spell for Panic on the Approach

I am She who filched the lispers of flux and who limptwisted the lady rejolt; I am feral and imposed on Damsel.

Diminished Prophecy

She will bring you to the cottage that belonged to your vestals, the ones who were spared. There you will select new color schemes and hang strands of fleshy beads. She will make you more guarded and sublime than all who spurted before.

Diminished Prophecy

Even if your spilling melds into dirt and twitches, tramped into crick by shady loves, from there the LORDESS your lune will swoop down and bucket your puddles.

Spell for Being Lukeswarmed into Any Scrape One May Fetish

I outlasted the woe-dodoness while the Ostrich-Goose untaught you to me. Hailworm to you, you who floozied up the skyracket, the wifeless, pining bird who gargles moontight meltnoun. I shall demyth you and I shall joyride the GOURD; maim way, so I may patter on.

Spell for Chasing the Wallows

I am She who nixed the eyelets from the fluttering text
that could not be sold and I am She who juggled between
Beau and Shepherd, Gigolo and Fishyman. Now I have
dumbed and approved the Tempest and Vale for entry
into my slumped chamber.

Spell for Sipping the Elixir

May the baited remedy be loosened for Damsel, may the
molten remedy of Vale and the remedy of Sultana be
unknown to the Higher Ache in this her name Czarina.
May I be askanted like the tail of Fishyman, for I am He
who lowdowned in the swamp, I am Gigolo of heyholla, I
am Miscreant who excreted the lore, the lore Apron used
to preheat the covenwhat, that mauled Woe-Dodo who
served me, bucketless lapse given to me, for I am She
who parroted buckets, to whom evercasting was given.

Spell for Ceasing the Pandering to the Daybroken Spiral

O sallow-hued beam who forflakes by supine rod and who limps on the slack, I will not be slack for you, I will not suture to you, your blood shall not brine into mine, for mine embered and calls herself Sea-Slag. If I am not slack for you, sucking coal from you, your blood shall not brine into mine. I am once upon a moancroak, my patronage comes from the torsos of minnows, the inception of Czarina who submerged into Sultana who emerged from Damsel who dined with Apron who served Woe-Dodo. I am She who was snatched by the Ostrich-Goose and clogtied into Bombshell by Harpy; I have moonwoke, I am the slighted Prophetess of GOURD, I am shroud-green and gloss!

Spell for Lunching After the Death

O Sunwurst who defined a moonmoan, O Sunwurst who
sleeps rainbows, may you deem worth within the argued
and past wooed, may those who are heartsick pardon
your slack and paw, may the netherwurst receive you
when Damsel enters stage bereft in Apron to blank your
weakish wishes in the torsos to the flinching bleats.

Spell for Not Dueling with Dead Loveswap

It is I who lispers in the tunnels of the Tempest who is slack; I have left Tabernacleville, I am guinea fig and soapstone, I am installed in the chambers of bunkers.

Spell for Sipping Elixir and Not Being Learnt by Sunwurst

O spoonswirl of Sunwurst, I am wrought with snot, for
I am bombswell from which the GOURD was sowed.
I will be neither learnt nor scored, for I am Prophetess,
eldest of the GOURD for who all the covegrunt trembles
with her EYE on Tabershrillville; I am the traversed
clairvoblunt when Damsel is lost in hoopskirt, my name
will carry furlong and a big wick.

Diminished Prophecy

For then there will be a marvelous letnoun, an unrivaled seamstress of prattle, the eclipse of the rotund Venus— never to rhyme again.

Spell For a Fountain Faker to be Settled on the Jugular of the Hierophant

O my Fishyman, my Shepard, my Harpy, remind me, keep watch, for I am Damsel of the GOURD who should be reminded of Gigolo's goggles.

To be awoken by a fountain faker swirled with bombswell tribed together—it is to be settled on the jugular of the hierophant on the eve of burial.

Spell For a Squat Token of Dread Stone

You halve your breastfed, O Harpy; you halve your tower,
O Harpy; you halve your tragic into marry, O Harpy.
The token is sentry for this wantonness which will revive
whomever attains autonomy despite.

A thugscrew; you shall not dragwept another Damsel for
there is pairing and poise.

Spell for Extinguishing Woe-Dodo

O you who consummated mental somersaults, prescribed
gash for me, remove the frowngown, for I am Sultana,
emerged from and feasted upon Fishyman, within he
teaches how to feed the minnows and ready the swamp. I
revived my torso from simp ash, ironed Apron when Vale
balked. Woe-Dodo, consumer of gloomporn, pyroassed
bootyshawl, let this water dissolve the flies you tend. I
am milestone and migraine, I walk with my torso, I speak
with confiscated flippers reclaiming the Higher Ache.

Another Spell for Extinguishing Woe-Dodo

I heartsored the eastered gland, I will not enlarge the
plate of depletion, nor ring the shanked baubledasses,
O they caressed! Because I evolved brass paramour into
the blitzed milked fray, shunned to whom the GOURD
tranced her scour into that decay when the bethrolined
towers aligned during the fish-turned-seal-turned-
hippopotamus pageant.

As for he who wallows in this spell, he will not swap me
for a spectre and he will never again feud funeral in the
realm of Damsel.

Diminished Prophecy

She scrolled this parafull: "Mind the shamwag and all his boundswell."

Spell for Noting the So-Called Herd

The legroom is tucked into the anchor, the half-bred
rubdown brines in the urn, the taste is digested and
she who distraught it, bought it. I note it, for I dreamed
into it by GOURD, and I never woke nor echoed to
the Vale. I traveled on husband to author legroom so to
dissolve into the anchor, to sip the brine in the urn and
to quell the taste for him who numbed it. I razed this
charm because of what I noted, I have not dreamed of
GOURD, I have not echoed to Vale.

Hey to you, So-Called Herd! Note that husbands long for
legroom which is a kind of taste drained at this meadow.
Recoup the appointment that is to be appointed.

I note the So-Called Herd. What is gray in the half-breed
and stalled in the full mask, that is written off.

Diminished Prophecy

If those wordplays had not ceased, she would have
humbled him to crumbs, but for the wake in his wrought
her flaresays tendrilled back down into her wrote.

Spell for Refunding Her Who Bozoed a Wineglass

Forget that, you Woe-Dodo whom Shepherd disputes, whose hedge Gigolo diseased! I dumped everything expired in restraint to you which said something about you with the mancatcher orphaned with fishing nets and dimwits.

Forget that, you whom Shepherd in the nether-barb disputes when he saves sound with a feral whine! Puree yourselves, all you gourds, spell and without mercy, cured of the inflected roam.

Forget that, you bozoer of a wineglass, whom Shepherd in the kinglet disputes! I typo, I typo, I typo, I type! Are you gawking? I'm heaving . . .

Diminished Prophecy

"Here is my musn't, whom I consoled, my cloven love whom I handsmite: I will assign him faultless and he will fetch hubris to serve beneath my tartness."

The Death of Woe-DoDo

eginning with the wailhouse of sickbeds, the sickbeds will conceal meanness from you. From the wailhouse of . . . . . will conceal mistreatment. Your trust will conceal time. The efforts of your seduction will conceal defeat. You withstood distance, you cannot withstand bareness.

Diminished Prophecy

A boozed linefeed will not bring dayache and a smirking classic will not puff on. In faithfulwaste he will ring the forrotten weirdness.

The Death of Dandy

"Let Dandy be host, beneath the helm of dreadbeds,
be the author of banterhole. Let him be punted to a
spectre, so that he will trespass jumbled and wrestle
verbiage, what he writes will be as bland as waving from
a turnipdove."

The Death of Gigolo

. . . blowgunned . . .

. . . of cured misname . . . . mismatched the torsos
with slips . . . . pulped her nightwear for slip.

The Death of Beau

With the beauscrew ignored, Beau misnamed bareness flawed with a (?) catchall manwhine. "You withstood distance, you cannot withstand bareness."

. . . Mildly humored and . . . a cackle . . . Without Beau (i.e. Name) . . . Harpy (hawk of invention), wife of Shameman, will peck his lines in this crawlspace of blamelessness.

The Death of Thingamabob

And when the far-flung mascot, Thingamabob, when his
heart choked . . . . his ides . . . . ! . . . a bloodseam . . .
. . . . . ! "Am I begone as an omen wormed . . . . . . on the
snap of my lone Apron? . . . . who mistakes treading
for grace (?)" . . . . . Tempest, with no trinkets or poems,
aches astray.

The Death of Miscreant

. . . . Pined and chorted . . . .
. . . . . elbowed, ... his askance. . . . . . . etched with
razored seams, ... his wafting toxins.

The Death of Vale

. . . Vale . . . drained Damsel's gown, he'll never writhe again . . . drained her gown and never to writhe again. He of wetsuited lip-wanking . . . drained her gown and is never to writhe again. He who houndscaped . . . drained her gown and is never to writhe again. The fleedung . . . drained her gown and is never to writhe again. He who was permitted to . . . and feasted on nooks drained her gown and is never to writhe again. The lure of achewalk drained her gown and is never to writhe again. He who stroked bedghost drained her gown and is never to writhe again. The faker of manstroked couplings drained her gown and is never to writhe again. He who blushed the mounds drained her gown and is never to writhe again. He drained her gown on his forebed and is never to writhe again. He drained her gown in the valley of fisheyes and will never writhe again.

Diminished Prophecy

He will not dither or be warpaged until he harbursts all
her worth. Mastering his defondled lessons she will cope.

The Tabernacle Hymns

our grave . . . violas made from stinkwood. Slimelight does not entwine your mealtime in the GOURD's stairwell, the grave . . . , the symmetrical. Your time-laced tower is sane and has no snatch. Your spectre, grave spectre, has fiddled fertile a hopeful clown for your predicament—O Dandy with a crowd spaced around your helm, ringing north jiving wornbushes, boorish wornbushes for the feast, O Thy Dandy, your time, your grave time!

Your spectre, grave spectre fable, the bentwood lore, the lore of the limptwist of hamstitch, the lore that ditched deadmate, the grave mound fable embossed a hound in your instinct, O canine snafu, tapering her seam through your debut.

Your spectre, the ghost dearness beaucoup, the ghost dearness is a wardrobe bored of bauble, a lemming ceasing praise. She is an oddbell stork bankrupting the groundswell. As wrong as explained, she adorns brushfiber. Dandy, sum of Tempest, embossed a hound in his instinct, O houndish karma, tapering its seam through your debut.

Diminished Prophecy

For the nobledolls will subsist snugger without khan
or Vale, without foreprank or nosebled crone, without
sparsely-doled jargon or muzzle.

A Hymn to Sultana

Razing her hemstitch, authoring with a snipping void,
vetoing the waistline pouching of the gourdchime, . . . of
the nightstand, she damsels through hellhoax and stylizes
past ruin.

A Hymn to Shepherd

. . . . . . barbwisked by chill, negated . . . . flunky
. . . . . . ; she plaited you . . . . . . she punned you into
your slap-pricked twist.

A Hymn to Damsel

Sideshow, weirdo, caustic syrup of GOURD,
backwashing like a rainswarm, forenumbed and dwelling.
Dense in tangent, unclear, purging the fluff, angry she
. . . . changes typeface; GOURD serves syrupy
weirdness, knotting her hairpiece, changing this hollow
strand, her lovetucked thorn . . . in the strand, struggling
. . . . . . with wellwashes.

Diminished Prophecy

My GOURD will refill them, because they snickered and
hindered; they will waddle nameless among the stumps.

Proverb 1

You should not concede to the foxcrock what was already conceded to the corndread.

Proverb 2

"Though I stitch with breastbone left lone, I will eject your breastbone!" Will this spear a shepherd to the howling of his pout?

Proverb 3

Don't allow the affair that paves you to become your expressway.

Proverb 4

Let his prickbed be cabbage . . . plagues, so that it
clobbers his turngoat.

Let his wetbed be . . . sawgroans so that it tricks his
dreamgoat.

Let his forebed be . . . heartbleat, so that it . . . his
ghostgoat.

He who wakes at night . . . cannot . . .

from The Forgiveness Canon

"He construed me, he sunstruck me, he renamed me, he rawboned me"—in hellos that tireslumed sunken hopes, hogwish shall never flinch.

"He construed me, he sunstruck me, he renamed me, he rawboned me"—in hellos that did not tireslum sunken hopes, hogwish shall flinch.

from The Forgiveness Canon

My Sultana, I scrapegrace all my goatskins to restore you.
In my extraction
They did not reserve mercy
But I task you
To forge your eyesores
To my gaunt blanket
And stitch it
To your supreme blanket.

Woeprinted you resolved
To supply my fishskin,
Graft onto me forwarning
For all whims.
Trespassed, I may not laud fiendstones
The birthwrought of my fishskin.
A birthwrought that nightdredges
Past meadows.

Absolve me, severe Sultana,
For I conspire to wittle heartwood
No clatter, nothing lusted.
Shake decay, decoy
And duly center
Spinwiped you bind in me
That is your cost

My righteous pill.

Severe Sultana, emboss me

So that I may decorate your ripening quilt.

The Epistle of Damsel

Magi, seer of Sea-Slag, to Damsel nee Woe-DoDo,
Miscreant, Apron, etc., who now travails in GOURD,
Hey:

2. I am versed, consoling you and your remedies, realized
without dose and haven

3. For it is chronicled that you ceased attachment with
the malign and fiend nee Shepherd, Beau, Gigolo,
Fishyman, Harpy, etc.,

and weaved the bombast and wicked into your own
elixired scribbles to uplift the defunct

4. Which when I perceived, I knew that either you are
Czarina herself weeped from the egged-eye of the lady
dragon or Sultana, daughter of the Higher Ache

5. On this unrest I inscribe, wholeheart and storm,
longing for your hornet, the stinger of verity, to join and
heal our deported bedrolls

6. For I hear Shepherd calls you cruel and Gigolo counts
you needy as Beau chants weird, all intending you unrest
with unfeeling

7. My metropolis is haul, but upbeat and expressive for the both of us

Magi

* * *

Magi, you are courtly, bunches you receive me, though we have not yet met

2. For it is revealed that those who bereave me do not recognize me, that they who do not grieve might beckon to only buckle

3. As to that invitation to your metropolis, I must relate regret and unmet expenses during this ongoing midstrife and that regret extends to all who once clutched me

4. But after my cocooning I will emit one of my dishtowels who will absorb your malaise and give wife to you, and to all who came along to clutch me

Damsel of GOURD

GOURD Has Remembered

his is what Prophetess of GOURD says—she who cremated the hemlouts and stressed everyone out, who sprained his mirth and all that succhums it, who gives mist to her nubs and nerve to those who stalk it:

"I, GOURD, have called you in consciousness; I will scold your wakeland. I will detain you and presswhore you into a covengrunt under the steeple and invite the Gentlepen."

In the cinched mumblings, Prophetess relinquished the lamented to Magi in his boomtown. To a versed mouth, pleasure in the ripened quilt, a segment of Czarina. The versed mouth was Damsel. The lamented consented and cried, "Grievance, you hyphenating fakers! Your reward is this myth."

"I am Prophetess's surcoat," Damsel added. "May I gleam as self and heartwould." Then the lament lessened.

This allowed the burst of genus to splice: her muzzle
Harpy straighedged her torso, mentored Shepherd
before he unraveled, Damsel swellbound with chide at
last construed his holey trinket. Beastly Shepherd, her
humdrunk and a write-off, edited his tricked scapegrace.
He refined remorse to a crumpet.

Each remiss unhooked lace to chenille, what Damsel
plead breakthrough and locket: The versed mouth
wished a chidebed and wished forgiveness for each
version. Midway Shepherd wished a conjure—which
meant: Gone within grayness.

When Shepherd wove slipup, he undid what the
lamented of Magi construed and mistook Damsel as
Apron. He halved heartprowl useless until she wished a
chidebed. And he waved fringeless, blamed sickness.

Diminished Prophecy

She will retool poems in hems lined with pompoms—
jump as I retrieve absurdity from my phonetics. I will
also gift her the morphine jar.

Diminished Prophecy

I wallowed as the lapse opined the worst of my sense and
seams. Again, I hurted whatnot like a bedsore lingering
creeper with a choice in void. I complied! I mistook
menswear for prayer and believed it a united course.
Thought writer spelled Beau, giver of gown and notice.
He swallowed a cauldron he mistook for a comma.

Diminished Prophecy

Wedded to the lapse, Apron shunned the ordeal, I
favored shunning the limpness, speaking the creeping
prayer: "Be gone lisping grayness! I already complied!"
When the next united course cased this place, it found a
wreckage. Its rhymer gimped pout, a tapered mouthpiece
from mirth: a rhymer discharged and abhorred.

Diminished Prophecy

When the lapse aproned the corner sequin, it hurt to absurd, a lingo shaded louse, "Weirdness!" I shook and somewhere ignored a bland sack. Its rhymer trolling threadbare and scathed shorthand. I hurted soundly like a void bluetongueing, "A consort of repeat is worth about a daisy for my hankie. Do not damn the recoil and hemline!"

Diminished Prophecy

And off went the lapse aproning the forgiving sheets.
I, in turn, hurting the rhyme as forgiveness failed to
adhere, "Toilsome!" Somewhere I took a fishtail by force.
Its rhymer claimed depth and history with a sidestep. We
were shriven and banter, our forgiveness lacked worth.
Shilled by word and smile, beaklike and worse.

Diminished Prophecy

In yen for an earnest kindred, a glint, a gem, a reflection, a mine minder, an esteemed knave hinged in cadence flung from a smocked canon: she crawled to the canon and smock, "Scrawl to me and reply faithful, you who is new, simmering on the brimstone from bloodbad and lapse. For the graveday of bloodbad has curdled. Hurray for this meadow sprung from wastepoem!"

Acknowledgments

he author would like to thank the editors of the following publications in which some poems from this collection first appeared: *32Poems, Absent, Action Yes,* the *American Poetry Review, Anti-, Boog City Reader, Caffeine Destiny, Coconut, CUE, Dead Mule School of Southern Literature, Delirious Hem,* the *Denver syntax, Eleven Eleven, The Equalizer,* FOURSQUARE, *Galatea Resurrects, Gargoyle, If Poetry Journal, Inch, The Jungle* (Rope-A-Dope Press), *MiPOesias, Moria, Night Train, No Tell Motel,* OCHO, *P.F.S. Post, Rooms Outlast Us, Spooky Boyfriend, West Wind Review* and *Wheelhouse Magazine.*

Gratitude to Mary Behm-Steinberg for designing the amazing cover and illustrations and to Jill Alexander Essbaum, Rebecca Loudon, Joel Patton and PF Potvin for their insights and editorial guidance.

Additional appreciation to William Allegrezza, Michael Ball, Tom Beckett, Hugh Behm-Steinberg, Jason Behrends, Aaron Belz, Julia Bloch, Dan Brady, Ryan Call, Grace Cavalieri, Lorna Dee Cervantes, Diane Cipa, Eduardo Corral, Shanna Compton, Bruce Covey, Laura Cronk, Jim Daniels, Susan Muaddi Darraj, Peter Davis, Jeffrey Eaton, Adam Deutsch, Steve Fellner, Adam Fieled, Wade Fletcher, Sunil Freeman, Jeannine Hall Gailey, Amy Gerstler, Scott Glassman, Ed Gordon, Anne Gorrick, Lea Graham, Kate Greenstreet, Amy Guth, Shafer Hall, Stacey Harwood, Ginger Heatter, Dave Housely, Charles Jensen, Wendi Kaufman, Collin Kelley, Amy King, Rauan Klassnik, Jennifer L. Knox, Kevin Larimer, David Lehman, Erica Livingston, Joseph Massey, Didi Menendez, Joe Milford, Dan Nester, Thisbe Nissen, Charles Orr, Danielle Pafunda, Shann Palmer, Karl Parker, Michael Parker, Deborah Poe, Derek Pollard, Megan Punschke, Moriah Purdy, Barbara Jane Reyes, Carly Sachs, Nic Sebastian, Kyle Semmel, Laurel Snyder, Jeremy Spencer, Nicole Steinberg, Eileen R. Tabios, Art Taylor, Maureen Thorson, Chris Tonelli, Cheryl A Townsend, Michael Quattrone, Julie Wakeman-Linn, Betsy Wheeler, Mike Young and Tommy Zurhellen for their support of *God Damsel* and/or No Tell Books.

As always, my thanks and eternal love to my husband, Chris, and son, Gideon.

Mary Behm-Steinberg's acknowledgment statement:

Each of the collages in this book are made of literally hundreds
of pieces fit together like a puzzle, some repeated and some one-
offs, and many individual images within a piece composed of
several pieces. Many are digitally painted as well. I appreciate how
hard anyone works on their art, and have tried to keep straight
the sources of any photos I didn't take myself. That said, if I used
something and so warped, mangled, or otherwise changed it as
to make it unrecognizable, I may not credit it. If it is in the public
domain, I may not credit it. Besides which, figuring out where the
famous image is, is part of the fun of puzzling out a collage. An
example of this is Dante Gabriel Rossetti's *Beata Beatrix*, one of my
favorite paintings. Rossetti is long dead, and I have no idea who
the person is on Wikimedia commons who posted the photo, but
they listed it as public domain and I thank them for it, as well as all
the other anonymous contributors and artists, living or dead, and
apologize to anyone I may have left out in credits.

Non-anonymous contributors include the amazing Reb Livingston,
who I am grateful to not just for the pumpkins and personal photos,
but for the opportunity to work on this fabulous book; my soulmate
Hugh Behm-Steinberg, not just for taking photos, but for holding
the icky rattlesnake head while I photographed it and putting up
with tantrums; Jill Alexander Essbaum, whose magnificent apples
saved my ass more than once on this project; Dan Haddick for
offering his fly; Howard F. Schwartz, Colorado State University for
an apple branch; Peacay of Bibliodyssey for endless inspiration and
leading me to the creative commons licenses for Christie's Auction
House (Dodo), Yale Beineke Library (Ripley Scroll), the University
of Strasbourg (botanicals); Lee of Tokyo Fish in Berkeley for letting
me photograph his amazing comestibles and even offering to pose
them for me; Monterey Market, the East Bay Vivarium, and the
Bone Room where I took yet more photos; NASA (moon); the
Smithsonian Belize larval fish project (listed as no known copyright,
no individual photographers listed). Thanks again to everyone who
in any way inspired any part of these collages.

About the Author

orn and raised in Pittsburgh, PA, Reb Livingston lives in Northern Virginia with her husband and son. She's the author of *Your Ten Favorite Words* (Coconut Books) and co-editor of *The Beside Guide to No Tell Motel* series. More information can be found at her website (reblivingston.net) and blog (reblivingston.blogspot.com).

Also by No Tell Books

2010

Glass is Really a Liquid, by Bruce Covey

Crushes, by Lea Graham

2009

PERSONATIONSKIN, by Karl Parker

2008

Cadaver Dogs, by Rebecca Loudon

2007

The Bedside Guide to No Tell Motel - 2nd Floor, editors Reb
       Livingston & Molly Arden

Harlot, by Jill Alexander Essbaum

Never Cry Woof, by Shafer Hall

Shy Green Fields, by Hugh Behm-Steinberg

The Myth of the Simple Machines, by Laurel Snyder

2006

The Bedside Guide to No Tell Motel, editors Reb Livingston
       & Molly Arden

Elapsing Speedway Organism, by Bruce Covey

The Attention Lesson, by PF Potvin

Navigate, Amelia Earhart's Letters Home, by Rebecca
       Loudon

Wanton Textiles, by Reb Livingston & Ravi Shankar

notellbooks.org